T5-CVJ-955

Animal Homes

by Sandra Widener

Orlando   Boston   Dallas   Chicago   San Diego

Visit *The Learning Site!*

www.harcourtschool.com

Animals need homes, just like people do. Sleepy animals need shelter. They want a safe, happy home.

Cliff swallows make mud nests that hold fast to old barns. The hot sun makes the muddy nests hard.

On windy days, swallows are safe in their nests up above.

Furry rabbits scurry. They nibble
plants in grassy places.

When they need shelter, the rabbits hurry to dig a den. The den can be used for years.

Snakes like rocky places in the sun.
They get sleepy in the warm sun.

On soggy or nasty days, snakes
look for shelter. They simply slip
into an empty crack in the earth.

River otters hurry to catch plenty of fish. Then the frisky otters play.

The otters make a sturdy den on the river. Part of the den is above the water. Part is under the water.

Animals make different homes. The homes are good for the ways they live. A snake would find an otter's home very wet and chilly.

No otter would want a snake's dusty home. Every animal is very happy in its own sturdy home.